Treasured Friends

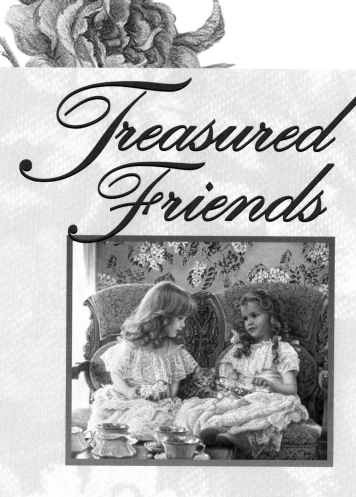

PAINTINGS BY
Sandra Kuck

TEXT BY
Heather Harpham Kopp

Harvest House Publishers
Eugene, Oregon 97402

Treasured Friends
Paintings by Sandra Kuck
Text by Heather Harpham Kopp

Copyright © 1996 by Harvest House Publishers
Eugene, Oregon 97402

ISBN 1-56507-445-9

Design and production by Garborg Design Works, Minneapolis, Minnesota

Harvest House Publishers has made every effort to trace the ownership of all quotes and poems in this book. In the event of any question from the use of any quote or poem, we regret any error made and will be pleased to make the necessary correction in future editions of this book.

Scripture quotations are from the Holy Bible, New International Version®, Copyright 1973, 1978, 1984 by the International Bible Society. Used by permission of Zondervan Publishing House.

Printed in Mexico.

96 97 98 99 00 01 02 03 04 05 // 10 9 8 7 6 5 4 3 2 1

To my friend

Sherry

On

Christmas Dec. 25, 1996

With love

Your friend always, Love, Kay

*Friendship is the golden thread
that ties the hearts of all the world.*

John Evelyn

The Best Sort to Have

*A friend
loves
at all
times.*

**The Book
of Proverbs**

When a friend looks out a window of your life, she sees the same world you do. Your happiness is her happiness. Your success is her success.

Such a friend is the best sort to have. Every good thing multiplies when it is shared by two with the same heart.

Friendship Hath a Lovely Face

A friend's face holds as many mysteries as the
stars. Her casual glances tell a hundred stories.
And in a friend's eyes and smile, you discover
your own strength. For when a friend tells
you the truth with kindness, you
remember her face forever.

My friend shall forever be my friend,
and reflect a ray of God to me.

Henry David Thoreau

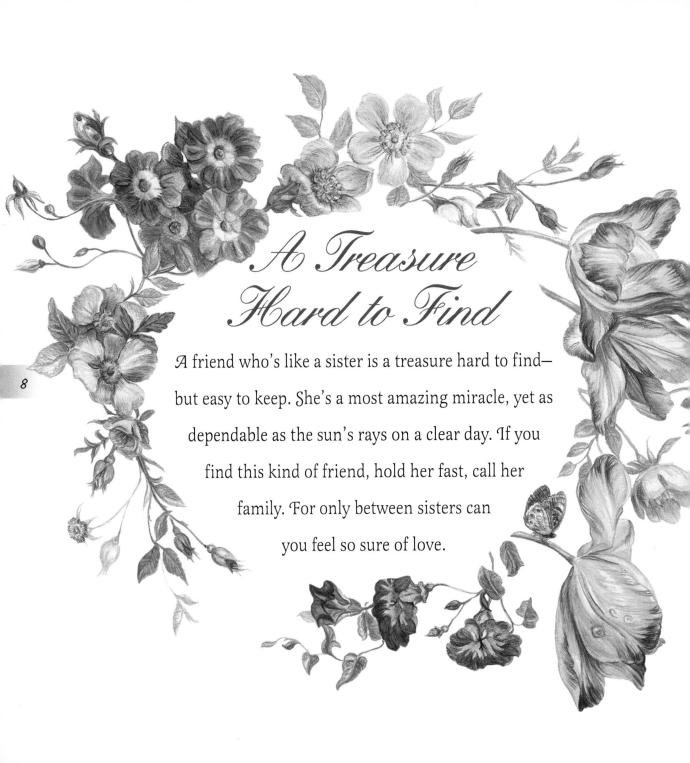

A Treasure Hard to Find

A friend who's like a sister is a treasure hard to find—but easy to keep. She's a most amazing miracle, yet as dependable as the sun's rays on a clear day. If you find this kind of friend, hold her fast, call her family. For only between sisters can you feel so sure of love.

Best of All

These are the things I prize

And hold of dearest worth:

Light of the sapphire skies,

Peace of the silent hills,

Shelter of the forest, comfort of the grass,

Music of birds, murmur of little rills,

Shadows of clouds that swiftly pass,

And, after showers,

The smell of flowers

And of the good brown earth—

And best of all, along the way, friendship and mirth.

Henry Van Dyke

Sharing Simple Wonders

A fiery sunset, tiny pansies by the wayside, the sound of raindrops tapping on the roof~what an extraordinary delight to share simple wonders with a true friend! With wide eyes and full hearts, you and I have come to cherish what others have missed.

Friendship is the breathing rose, with sweets in every fold.

Oliver Wendell Holmes

Friends Again

A quarrel with a friend lies so heavy on the heart.

When we were small, such squabbles could be solved

by a folded note of apology, a hesitant call to come for

lemonade on the swing—or even by our mothers!

Often we were reconciled by mere laughter. We would

burst out with mirth and merry all at once, and then

it seemed silly to be sad or angry again.

Then as now, there's always a way to make amends.

And after hurts have been heard, and tea set for two,

true friends still know how to say, "I forgive you."

The First Blush of Friendship

The first blush of friendship is a grace to behold: a moment of shyness, a tentative hello. Every other gift in life takes wing from here—affection, generosity, sharing—until soon your life is rich.

We cannot tell the precise moment when friendship is formed. As in filling a vessel drop by drop, there is at last a drop which makes it run over; so in a series of kindnesses there is at last one which makes the heart run over.

James Boswell

When the Day Is Through

Friendship—our friendship—is like the beautiful shadows of evening, spreading and growing till life and its light pass away.

Michael Vitkovics

Our dearest friends are best for do-nothing days. You can spend an afternoon, every hour, every moment of it together—and still have nothing at all to tell when the day is through.

Such friends savor a sweet, effortless friendship, nearly invisible—and altogether at peace.

The Miracle of Friendship

There's a miracle called friendship

That dwells within the heart,

And you don't know how it happens

Or where it gets its start.

But the happiness it brings you

Always gives a special lift,

And you realize that friendship

Is life's most precious gift.

Anonymous

Beautiful by the Way

A friend makes you beautiful—not just by her fashion suggestions or make-up tips. Not by how she brushes your hair or picks out the perfect dress for you. And not even because she wishes she had the gold flecks in your eyes, and tells you so.

A friend's reassurances go deeper than this. When she is close, you feel somehow more true, more sure of who you were always supposed to be. A friend makes you beautiful by the way she sees your soul.

How Sweet the Sound

Who knows how it starts? Your friend catches your eye at

just the right moment, and suddenly, almost magically, the

silliest thoughts pass between you.

How sweet the sound of

friends laughing

together, of sharing the joy

of knowing each other so well.

Pleasant words are a honeycomb, sweet to the soul and healing to the bones.

The Book of Proverbs

The Happy Ending

Some days we all feel like Cinderella—

our dreams unreachable, our true self

hidden from view.

Until a friend comes along. "You're beautiful," she

says. "You can be anything, do anything you want."

How happy the ending that makes us hope again.

How magical the friend who turns our doubts into

endless possibilities.

Friends...they cherish each other's hopes. They are kind to each other's dreams.

Henry David Thoreau

27

Lonely Is Longest

Lonely is longest when your friend goes away. But when she finally comes back—such sweet reunion! How blessed is she who leaves on occasion, but whose friendship remains constant.

Because of a friend, life is a little stronger, fuller, more gracious thing for the friend's existence, whether…near or far.…If the friend is…far away he still is there to think of, to wonder about, to hear from, to write to, to share life and experience with, to serve, to honor, to admire, to love.

Whispered Blessings

The loving words of a friend live on. Her kind advice rings true, and her amazing way of knowing when to say nothing at all is a most precious gift.

Even in her absence, her ideas and thoughts are always with you, like whispered blessings at just the right moment.

No love, no friendship can cross the path of our destiny without leaving some mark on it forever.

Francois Mauriac

I count myself in
nothing else so happy
As in a soul remembering
my good friends.

William Shakespeare